A VIKING TOWN

Series Editor	David Salariya
Book Editor	Jenny Millington

Author:
Fiona Macdonald studied history at Cambridge University and at the University of East Anglia, where she is a part-time tutor. She has written many books for children on historical topics, including *A Roman Fort, A 16th-Century Mosque* and *A Samurai Castle* in this series.

Illustrator:
Mark Bergin was born in Hastings in 1961. He studied at Eastbourne College of Art and specializes in historical reconstruction. He has illustrated a number of books in this series, including *A World War II Submarine, A Medieval Castle* and *A Greek Temple.*

Created, designed and produced by
The Salariya Book Co Ltd, Brighton, UK

First published in 1995
by Macdonald Young Books

Macdonald Young Books Ltd
Campus 400
Maylands Avenue
Hemel Hempstead
Herts
HP2 7EZ

C6056 36799
Cr,
/3948

ISBN 0-7500-1585-3

A catalogue record for this book is available from the British Library.

Printed and bound in Portugal by Edições ASA

A VIKING TOWN

FIONA MACDONALD   MARK BERGIN

MACDONALD YOUNG BOOKS

CONTENTS

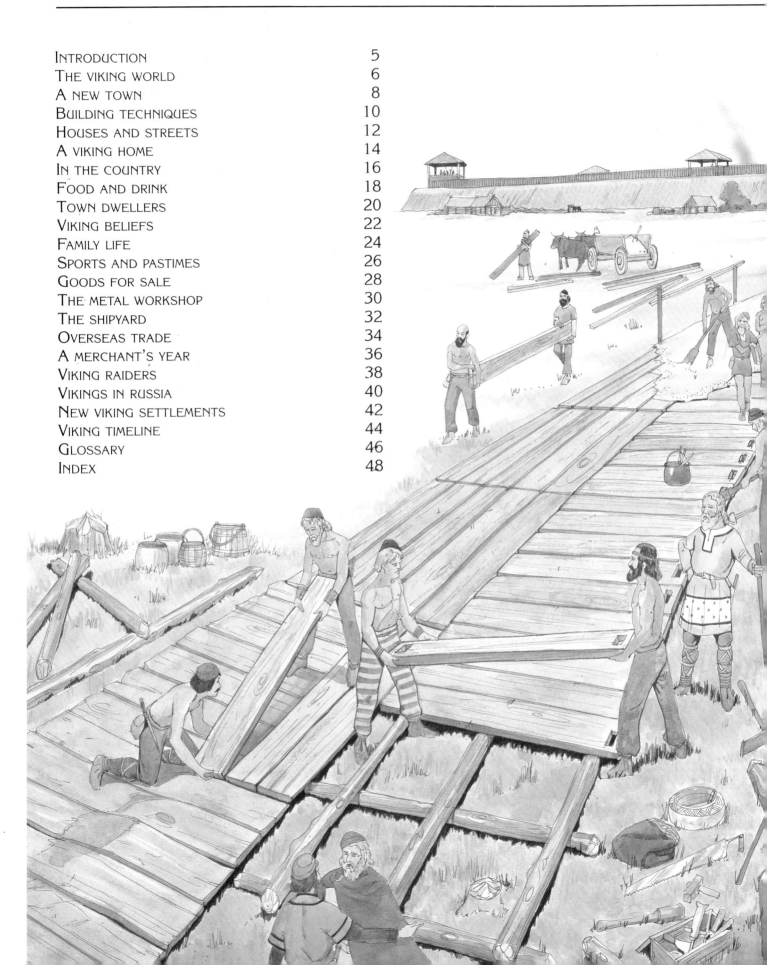

INTRODUCTION

Who were the Vikings? Brave warriors, dealing death and destruction to their enemies? Ruthless pirates, raiding tranquil monasteries and lonely farms?

Some Vikings did live like this, but they were a minority. The Viking civilisation flourished in Scandinavia (present-day Norway, Sweden and Denmark) from around AD 800 to 1100. Most Vikings lived peacefully at home in these lands, fishing, farming, hunting and gathering wild foods. Viking men were skilful craftworkers, making beautiful objects out of metal, wood and bone. Viking women were clever weavers and embroiderers, producing fine, warm fabrics of linen and wool.

Many Viking families were self-sufficient, growing all their own food and making all the clothes, tools and furniture they needed for themselves. But other families were not. They grew food or made goods to sell, either to country traders, who tramped from village to village, buying and bartering all sorts of local produce, or else to rich international merchants who travelled long distances to buy top-quality Viking craft goods.

In many parts of the Viking homelands, kings and lords protected thriving country markets and busy trading towns. The most famous were at Kaupang in Norway, Birka in Sweden and Hedeby in Schleswig (today this is part of Germany, but then it was ruled by Denmark). What was life like there? You can find out more from this book.

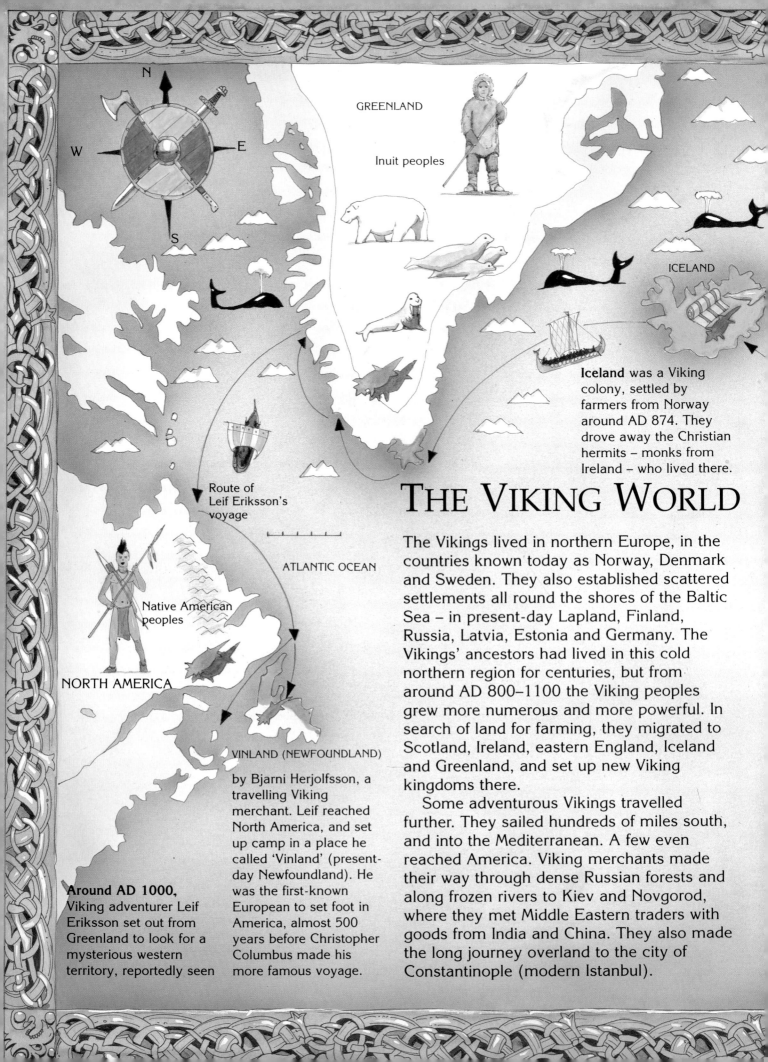

GREENLAND

Inuit peoples

ICELAND

N

W   E

S

Iceland was a Viking
colony, settled by
farmers from Norway
around AD 874. They
drove away the Christian
hermits – monks from
Ireland – who lived there.

Route of
Leif Eriksson's
voyage

ATLANTIC OCEAN

Native American
peoples

NORTH AMERICA

VINLAND (NEWFOUNDLAND)

THE VIKING WORLD

The Vikings lived in northern Europe, in the
countries known today as Norway, Denmark
and Sweden. They also established scattered
settlements all round the shores of the Baltic
Sea – in present-day Lapland, Finland,
Russia, Latvia, Estonia and Germany. The
Vikings' ancestors had lived in this cold
northern region for centuries, but from
around AD 800–1100 the Viking peoples
grew more numerous and more powerful. In
search of land for farming, they migrated to
Scotland, Ireland, eastern England, Iceland
and Greenland, and set up new Viking
kingdoms there.

Some adventurous Vikings travelled
further. They sailed hundreds of miles south,
and into the Mediterranean. A few even
reached America. Viking merchants made
their way through dense Russian forests and
along frozen rivers to Kiev and Novgorod,
where they met Middle Eastern traders with
goods from India and China. They also made
the long journey overland to the city of
Constantinople (modern Istanbul).

Around AD 1000,
Viking adventurer Leif
Eriksson set out from
Greenland to look for a
mysterious western
territory, reportedly seen
by Bjarni Herjolfsson, a
travelling Viking
merchant. Leif reached
North America, and set
up camp in a place he
called 'Vinland' (present-
day Newfoundland). He
was the first-known
European to set foot in
America, almost 500
years before Christopher
Columbus made his
more famous voyage.

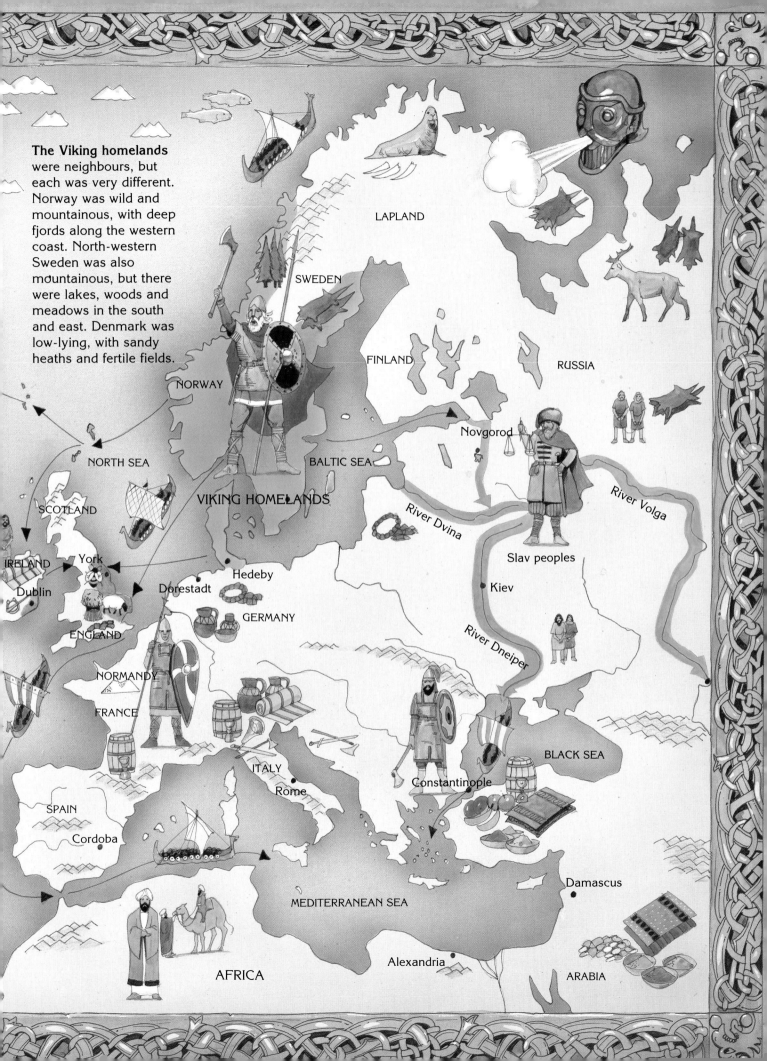

The Viking homelands were neighbours, but each was very different. Norway was wild and mountainous, with deep fjords along the western coast. North-western Sweden was also mountainous, but there were lakes, woods and meadows in the south and east. Denmark was low-lying, with sandy heaths and fertile fields.

LAPLAND

SWEDEN

FINLAND

RUSSIA

NORWAY

Novgorod

NORTH SEA

BALTIC SEA

River Dvina

River Volga

VIKING HOMELANDS

SCOTLAND

Slav peoples

IRELAND

York

Kiev

Dublin

Hedeby

Dorestadt

River Dneiper

ENGLAND

GERMANY

NORMANDY

FRANCE

BLACK SEA

ITALY

Rome

Constantinople

SPAIN

Cordoba

Damascus

MEDITERRANEAN SEA

AFRICA

Alexandria

ARABIA

A New Town

At first sight, the area around Hedeby did not look like an ideal place to build a new town. To the west lay marshland, where slow, winding rivers overflowed their banks. To the east lay a bleak, windswept estuary, leading to the bitter Baltic Sea. Just north of the town lay a hill fort, keeping watch over the heath. This was border country – hostile German tribes were never far away. Until the early 9th century, Hedeby was not much more than a few scattered hamlets, down by the sea.

But there was something else about the site of Hedeby, far more important than all its natural disadvantages. It lay at the junction of two international trading routes. Rich travellers from many lands frequently passed by. Tenth-century chronicles report that this potentially profitable fact was recognised by King Godfred of Denmark. They tell how in AD 808 he moved a group of Viking merchants to Hedeby from the Slav town of Reric, and encouraged them to set up a new trading centre there.

Hedeby was built where two important trade routes crossed. One led north–south, from Germany to Scandinavia; the other led east–west, from the North Sea to the Baltic, cutting off a long, risky journey by sea around the northern tip of Denmark. Hedeby originated from several small settlements on neighbouring sites, and gradually grew into a major trading and manufacturing centre. Like all Viking towns, Hedeby was well-guarded.

It is hard to be certain whether the old chroniclers were telling the truth. But Hedeby's layout was so neatly planned, and so many workmen would have been needed to build it, that archaeologists think it was probably constructed – or, at least, rebuilt around some smaller, earlier settlements – on the orders of a rich, powerful king.

The walls surrounding Hedeby were made of closely-packed earth, heaped into a steep, sloping bank. It was topped by a strong palisade – a wall made of thick tree trunks driven into the ground.

Gates were 'tunnels' in the walls, guarded by lookouts in watch-towers.

Watchtower

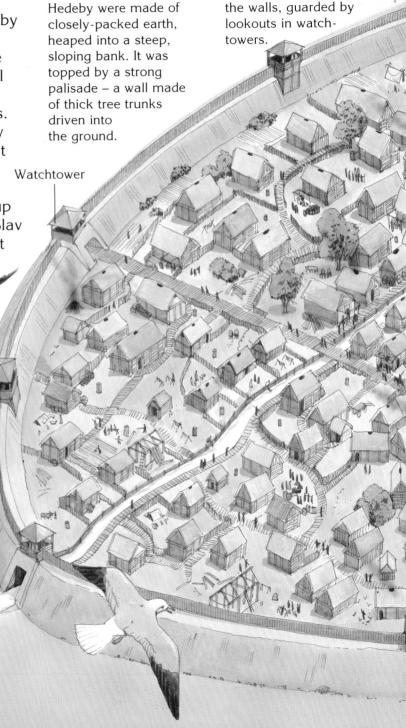

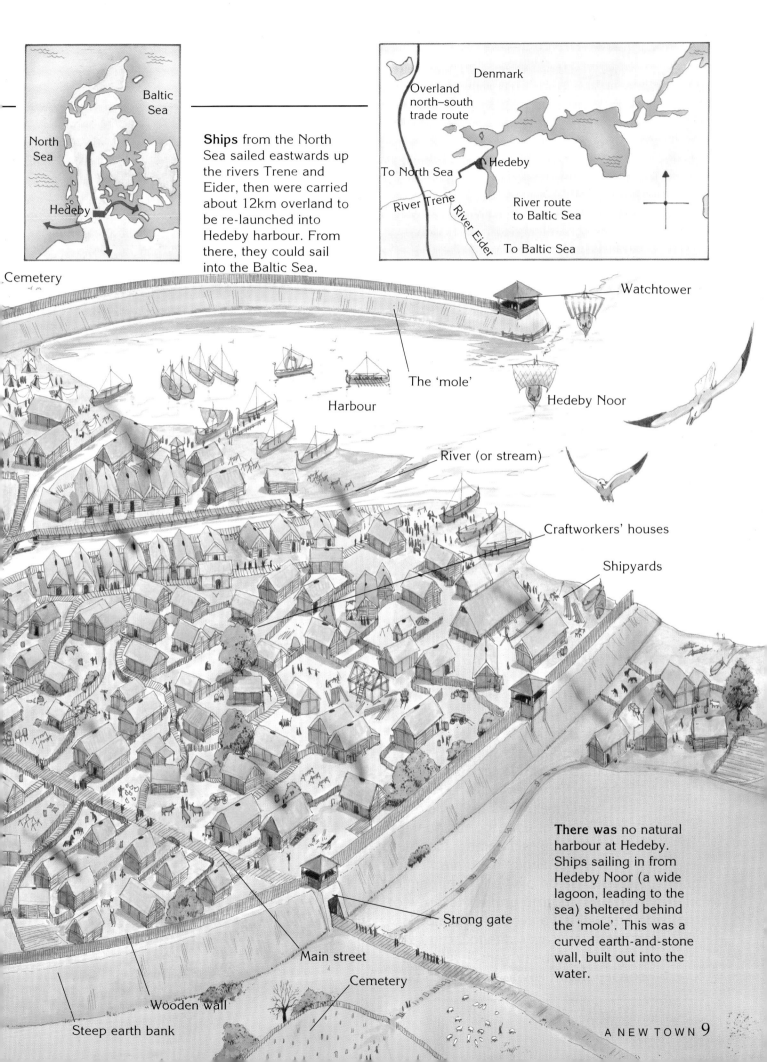

Baltic Sea

North Sea

Hedeby

Ships from the North Sea sailed eastwards up the rivers Trene and Eider, then were carried about 12km overland to be re-launched into Hedeby harbour. From there, they could sail into the Baltic Sea.

Denmark

Overland north–south trade route

To North Sea

Hedeby

River route to Baltic Sea

River Trene

River Eider

To Baltic Sea

Cemetery

Watchtower

The 'mole'

Harbour

Hedeby Noor

River (or stream)

Craftworkers' houses

Shipyards

Strong gate

There was no natural harbour at Hedeby. Ships sailing in from Hedeby Noor (a wide lagoon, leading to the sea) sheltered behind the 'mole'. This was a curved earth-and-stone wall, built out into the water.

Main street

Cemetery

Wooden wall

Steep earth bank

A NEW TOWN 9

BUILDING TECHNIQUES

Like many Viking settlements in lowland countries, Hedeby was built from wood and earth. There was no suitable stone nearby. Huge earth mounds were heaped up to make walls; by the 10th century, they reached 10 metres high. Whole forests of timber were felled to build watchtowers and fences, or to lay wooden walkways across the shifting, sandy ground.

By Viking standards, the town was vast. About 24 hectares lay within its walls. There were some open areas, but most of the space was built-up. Houses were made of wood, and thatched with reeds. Walls could be either 'stave-built', that is, made of wedge-shaped vertical planks, or weather-boarded – made of overlapping horizontal boards. Cheaper homes had walls of wattle and daub. There were no chimneys, so smoke from fires escaped either through a hole in the roof, or, more usually, through a smoke hole in a gable end. This gave better protection from wind, rain and snow. All Hedeby houses were single-storey. And most – even the best and strongest – had to be rebuilt every 20 or 30 years. They had no foundations, but were built directly on the damp ground. Their timber frame, which supported walls and roof, soon rotted away.

Left:
Building a house. In lowland Viking countries, where there were trees to provide timber for building, houses were made of wood. They were constructed around a box-shaped timber frame. Triangular rafters were added to make a roof, which was thatched with reeds or straw. Walls were made of wattle-and-daub, or of vertical wooden planks. Some houses were built with double-thick walls to keep out the cold.

Wattle-and-daub walls: (Above) Weave hazel twigs in between upright poles. (Below) Cover woven walls with sticky clay and straw.

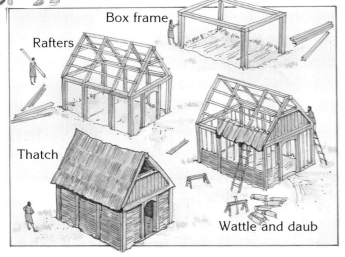

Box frame

Rafters

Thatch

Wattle and daub

Thatching: (Above) Arrange bundles of reeds across battens. (Below) Use bent hazel twigs to hold them down.

Below:
Making a raised walkway. First, drive tree-trunk piles into the soft ground. Use these piles to support strong cross-bars.

Now fix more tree-trunks and thick branches lengthways on top of the cross-bars. Hold them in place with heavy iron nails.

Finally, lay planks of wood crossways over the trunks and branches. Add rails on either side to stop horses and carts falling over the edge.

Wooden pile

Cross-bar

Supporting planks

Walkway

Farm animals in town

Barn

Leather curing

Fish drying

Wealthy citizen's house

Most houses, even in towns, had fenced-off plots of land where families kept chickens, pigs and cows to provide eggs, meat and milk.

HOUSES AND STREETS

Hedeby's wealthiest inhabitants – who were merchants and craft-workers – lived in the centre of town in well-built homes facing the busiest streets. They could afford spacious plots of land, so their houses were set back a little way and surrounded by wattle fences, for privacy and security. Storage sheds and workshops were built close by. Merchants and craft-workers did not usually keep much livestock – perhaps just a few chickens, a cat (to chase rats and mice away from valuable goods) and a guard dog. However, there were a few farmhouses, with stables, cattle-stalls and barns, towards the outskirts of the town.

An average merchant's house measured 6 metres wide by 15 metres long. Inside, it might have two or three rooms; the largest contained a hearth in the centre. Some houses also had separate clay ovens for baking bread – these would have provided welcome extra heating, too. Many wealthy Hedeby houses had their own wells.

Poor citizens lived in simpler, smaller homes: wattle-and-daub single-room huts built over a sunken pit, about 3 metres wide by 3 metres long, with a smoky hearth in the corner. Houses like this, built far beyond the prosperous centre of the town, must have been cold and damp in winter.

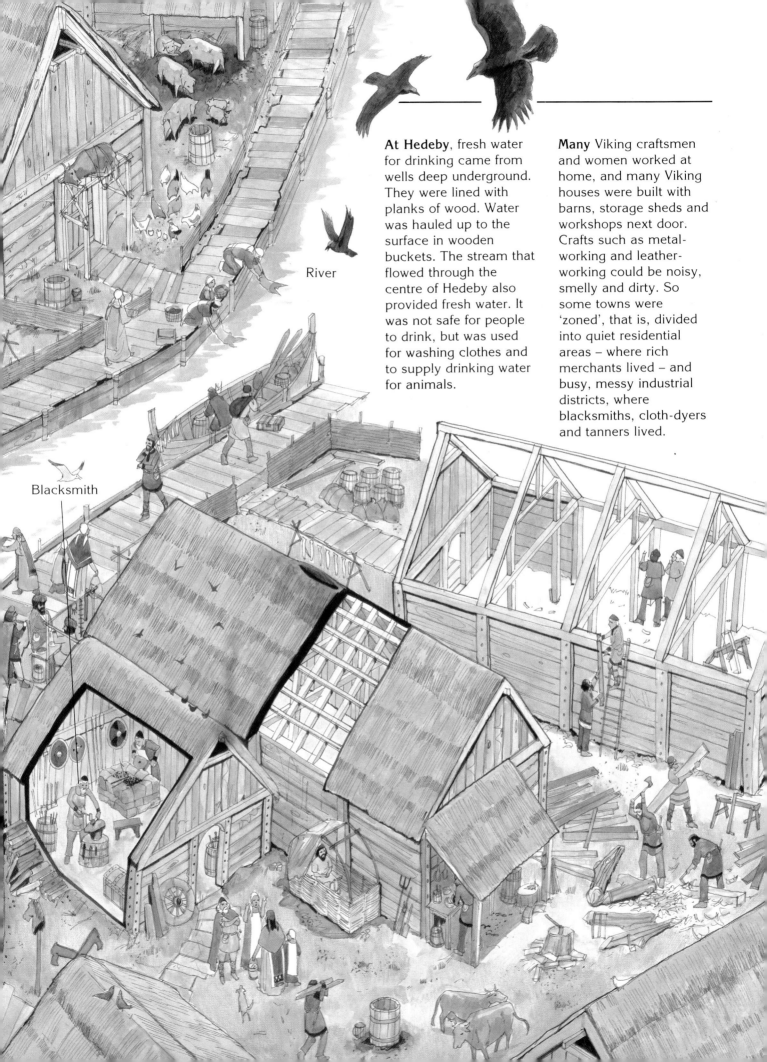

River

Blacksmith

At Hedeby, fresh water for drinking came from wells deep underground. They were lined with planks of wood. Water was hauled up to the surface in wooden buckets. The stream that flowed through the centre of Hedeby also provided fresh water. It was not safe for people to drink, but was used for washing clothes and to supply drinking water for animals.

Many Viking craftsmen and women worked at home, and many Viking houses were built with barns, storage sheds and workshops next door. Crafts such as metal-working and leather-working could be noisy, smelly and dirty. So some towns were 'zoned', that is, divided into quiet residential areas – where rich merchants lived – and busy, messy industrial districts, where blacksmiths, cloth-dyers and tanners lived.

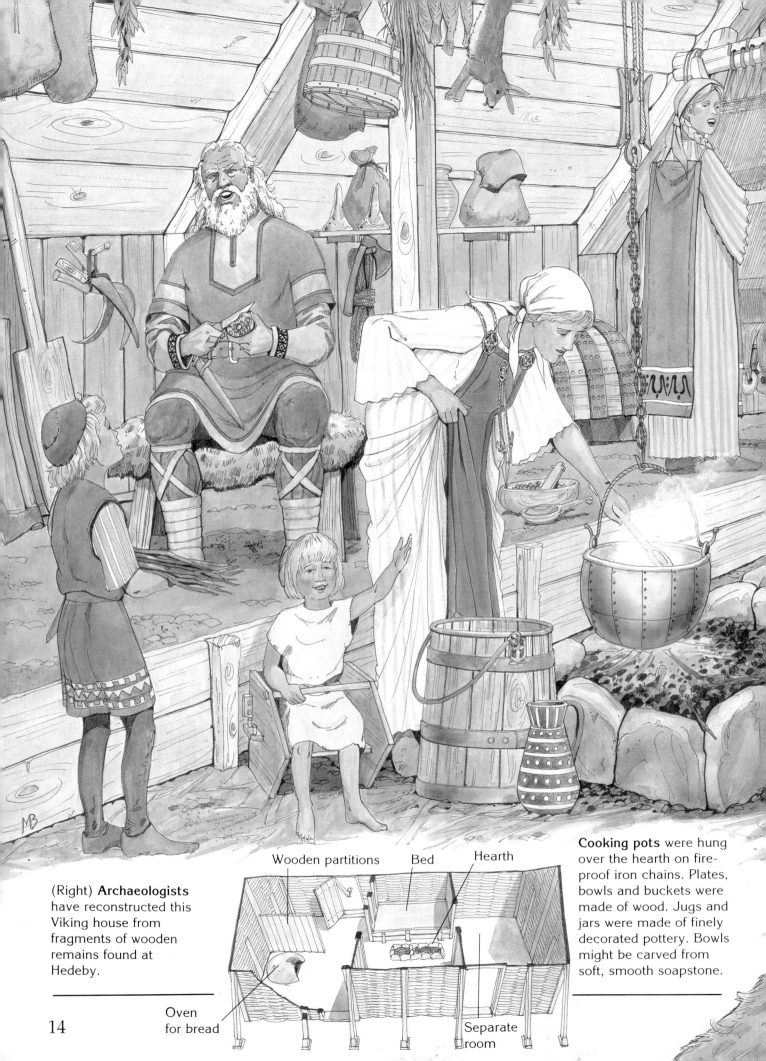

Cooking pots were hung over the hearth on fire-proof iron chains. Plates, bowls and buckets were made of wood. Jugs and jars were made of finely decorated pottery. Bowls might be carved from soft, smooth soapstone.

(Right) **Archaeologists** have reconstructed this Viking house from fragments of wooden remains found at Hedeby.

Wooden partitions

Bed

Hearth

Oven for bread

Separate room

A VIKING HOME

Weaving loom

Wool fleece

Distaff

Spindle

Thread

Viking houses were crowded and busy. They were workplaces, as well as somewhere to shelter and relax. All available space was used – for cooking, eating, sleeping, playing children's games, entertaining visitors, cleaning and polishing weapons, repairing farm tools, spinning, weaving, mending and embroidery.

In the summer, most of these activities could take place outside, but in winter, when snow lay all around and the sun did not rise until late morning, family, servants and slaves all stayed indoors, as close as they could to the fire. There were no windows to let in fresh air, so even the best-run homes were sometimes smelly, although the Vikings used outside lavatories, and took regular baths. Inside a Viking home, there was not much furniture. Everyone who could afford it had comfortable cushions and colourful wall-hangings – which also kept out draughts. Food was stored in pottery jars and wooden barrels, and clothes were folded away in chests. For sleeping, feather mattresses and woollen blankets were laid out on a low platform; only the richest homes had beds. In wealthy homes there might also be a separate sleeping area, partitioned off from the living room by a thin wall.

Wealthy Viking families could afford handsome, comfortable wooden furniture, like this splendid bed, with posts carved in the shape of animal heads. A similar bed was found at a Viking burial-site at Oseberg, in Norway. Archaeologists believe that the Viking queen Asa was buried there. In less wealthy homes, beds were much simpler – just a plain wooden 'box', filled with bracken or straw. In all houses, rich or poor, beds were built close to the hearth, for warmth on cold winter nights.

IN THE COUNTRY

The great Viking towns – Hedeby in Denmark, Birka in Sweden and Kaupang in Norway – played an important part in international trade. Other, smaller Viking towns were also important – as fishing ports, hideouts for raiders, or ship-building harbours. Even so, the majority of Vikings lived and worked in the countryside, as farmers, hunters and trappers, producing food for themselves and for the people who lived in towns. Meat, butter, cheese, grains, fruit and vegetables were all in demand.

Viking town craft-workers also depended on country skills; in remote valleys, iron smelters and charcoal burners prepared essential raw materials (iron 'bloom' and charcoal) for blacksmiths to use. Wool for townswomen to spin and weave came from flocks of mountain sheep. Furs for hats and cloaks, and deerskins for shoes and harnesses came from the northern forests. So did wood for houses and ship-building, tar for waterproofing, and beautiful, shiny amber for jewellery.

In late spring (May and June), men and boys climbed steep cliffs to gather eggs from the sea-birds nesting there.

Where the land was steep and rocky, country people made a living from the sea. Salt fish, whale oil, sealskin and walrus ivory could all be sold to travelling country merchants, who carried them to the towns for re-sale in the markets there.

Summer was the time to go whaling. Bands of hunters set out to spear whales at sea, or to kill them by driving them ashore.

In winter, seals were hunted as they rested on ice floes, or sometimes caught using fish bait lowered through holes cut in the ice.

All kinds of deer were hunted for their meat, hides, bones and antlers. Reindeer could be tamed and trained to pull sleds.

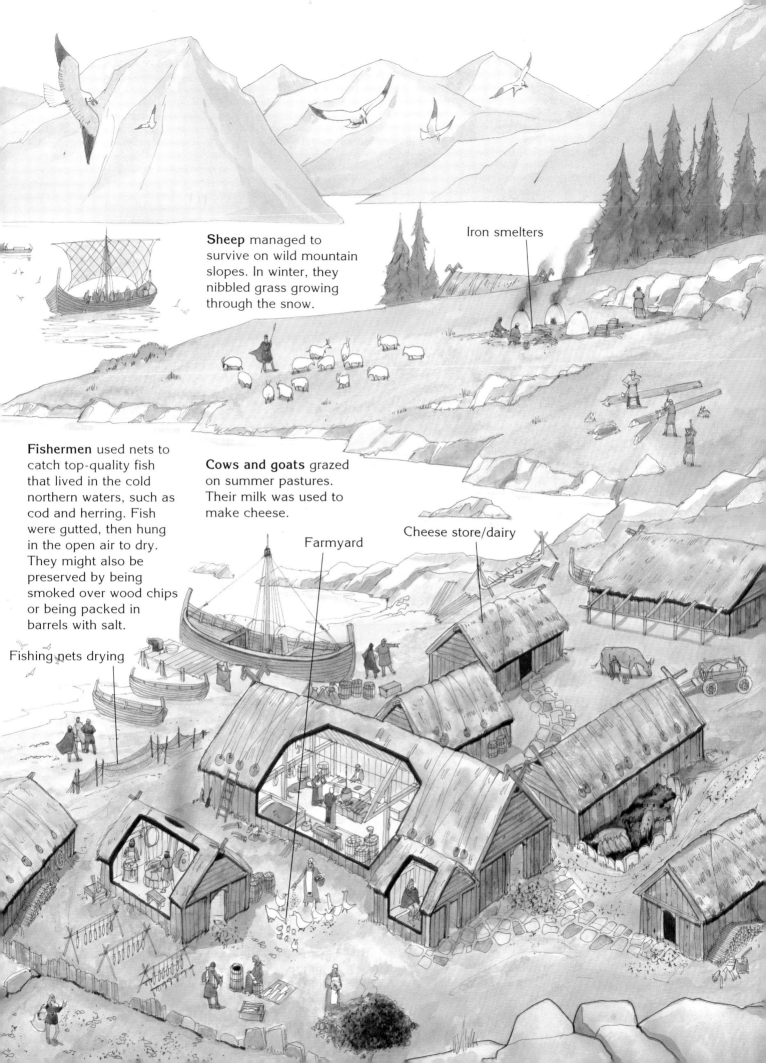

Sheep managed to survive on wild mountain slopes. In winter, they nibbled grass growing through the snow.

Iron smelters

Fishermen used nets to catch top-quality fish that lived in the cold northern waters, such as cod and herring. Fish were gutted, then hung in the open air to dry. They might also be preserved by being smoked over wood chips or being packed in barrels with salt.

Cows and goats grazed on summer pastures. Their milk was used to make cheese.

Cheese store/dairy

Farmyard

Fishing nets drying

FOOD AND DRINK

Living in cold northern lands, the Vikings knew that supplies of food could not be guaranteed. If the summer was wet, their crops might rot in the fields. If the hay in their barns went mouldy, their cows would not survive the winter. Sometimes there were famines, when strong men and women fainted from hunger, and old people and children were killed, so that precious food would not be 'wasted' on them.

Kitchen equipment:
1. Soapstone bowl.
2. Wooden ladle.
3. Frying-iron.
4. Iron spoon.
5. Iron fork.
6. Iron skewer.
7. Steel spark-striker, rubbed against a flint to make spark to light fires.
8. Iron toaster.

Cooking was women's work. Girls were taught by their mothers how to cook. They might also learn from helping well-trained women servants.

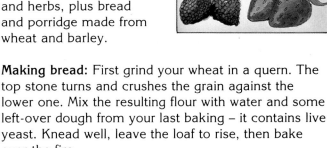

(Left) **Vikings** enjoyed meat and fish when they could get it. But hunters and fishermen could not expect a lucky catch every time they set out. (Right) The Viking diet included wild fruit, nuts and herbs, plus bread and porridge made from wheat and barley.

Fortunately, famines did not often occur. For the rest of the time, in towns and in the country, what you ate and drank depended on how rich you were. All but the very poorest people ate bread, fish, eggs, cheese and porridge. Wealthy Vikings also liked a lot of meat, especially baked or roasted. Viking cooks – housewives and their female servants – also made stews by digging a hole in the ground, filling it with water, adding meat, herbs and salt, then boiling everything together by dropping in red-hot stones. You could cook a leg of lamb in three hours this way.

Vikings drank ale (brewed from malted grain) or fresh spring water. Rich Vikings also liked expensive, imported wine, which came from the Rhineland in Germany. On special occasions, women brewed mead from honey and herbs. It was rumoured to have magical effects.

Making bread: First grind your wheat in a quern. The top stone turns and crushes the grain against the lower one. Mix the resulting flour with water and some left-over dough from your last baking – it contains live yeast. Knead well, leave the loaf to rise, then bake over the fire.

Feasts were held to welcome guests, celebrate family occasions such as weddings, or at special times of year, like the winter solstice.

Town Dwellers

This jarl can afford a fine woollen tunic with embroidered borders, and a thick cloak. In winter, he will wear furs. He carries a magnificent sword, and a purse full of silver coins.

Fur-trimmed hat

Woollen cap

Ring-and-pin brooch

Battle axe

Metal helmet

Plaited beard for battle

Tunic

Purse

Wide breeches

Dagger

Sword

Embroidery

Chain mail

Wood and leather shield

Leggings bound with strips of cloth

Leather shoes

This travelling merchant is wearing Slav-style baggy trousers and hat. Vikings captured the Slav peoples of eastern Europe to sell as slaves. Our modern word 'slave' comes from their name.

Viking clothes had to be weatherproof. Men and women wore thick

knitted socks. Leather for shoes was waterproofed with seal blubber.

Warriors wore chain mail armour or thick leather jerkins, and carried helmets, shields and swords.

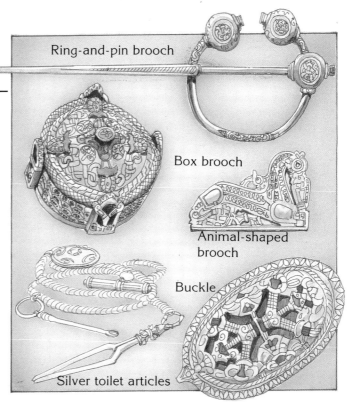

Ring-and-pin brooch

Box brooch

Animal-shaped brooch

Buckle

Silver toilet articles

Men and women liked to wear jewellery. It looked good, and displayed their wealth. This necklace is made of glass beads, gem-stones and fragments of finely-worked silver.

Men pinned their cloaks with ring brooches. Rich women wore buckles to fasten their tunics, and box brooches with beauty aids like tweezers hanging on silver chains.

Scarf

Buckle

Short cloak

Tunic

Pleated dress

Embroidered trim

Viking women wore several layers of clothing for warmth. First, a long dress of linen or wool, then an over-tunic, then a cloak. They might wear loose trousers underneath their dress. Married women covered their hair with a scarf.

Who lived in Viking towns? Mostly craft-workers and traders, together with people such as butchers, bakers, builders and money-changers, who were useful to them or their businesses. There might be a few farmers and perhaps a few fishermen, too. Evidence from Kaupang in Norway reveals hardly any permanent house-sites, just rows and rows of merchants' stalls. There were certainly houses at Hedeby, but excavations in the town's cemeteries show that many important people in Viking society, such as kings and jarls (lords), were missing from the community. They might visit the town, and offer it protection by their warriors, but they did not live and die there. In early Viking towns, priests, monks and nuns were often absent, too. In 827, a Christian missionary called Ansgar built a church at Hedeby, but he did not make many converts.

Some town-dwellers were rich, but others were very poor. Rich citizens lavished their money on magnificent display. Viking men as well as women enjoyed wearing fine, fur-trimmed clothes and eye-catching jewellery. Rich men also liked expensive, well-made armour and swords. But an old Viking story tells how poor people, unfree servants and slaves had to make do with tattered cast-off clothes.

VIKING BELIEFS

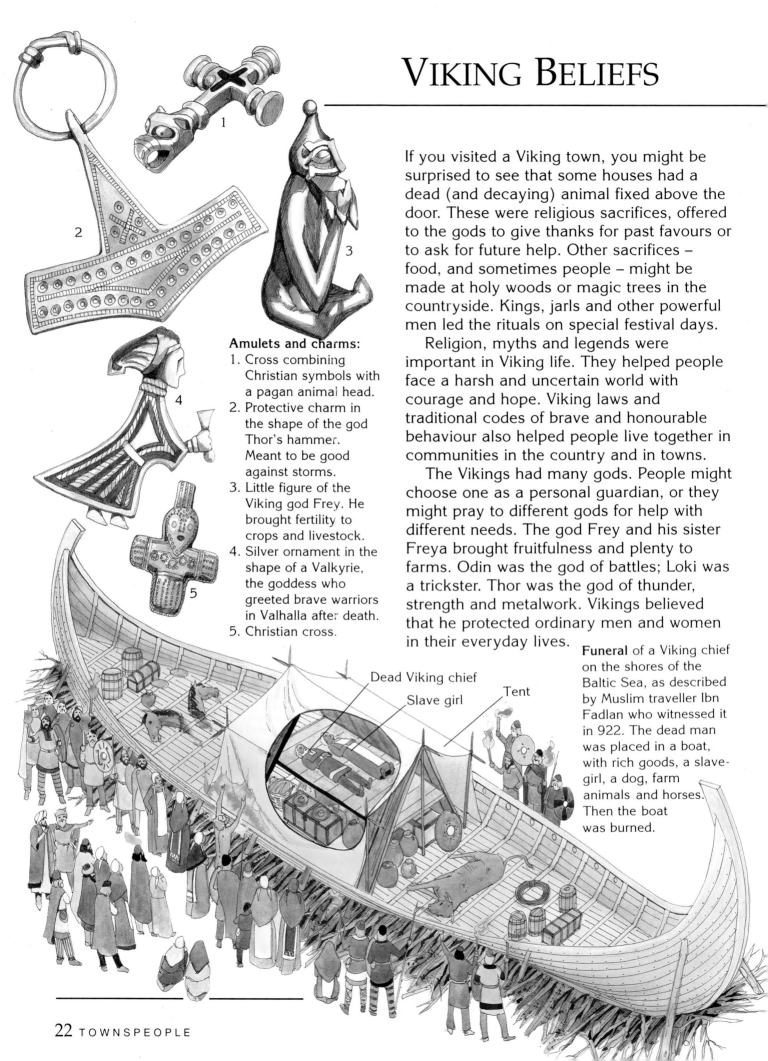

Amulets and charms:
1. Cross combining Christian symbols with a pagan animal head.
2. Protective charm in the shape of the god Thor's hammer. Meant to be good against storms.
3. Little figure of the Viking god Frey. He brought fertility to crops and livestock.
4. Silver ornament in the shape of a Valkyrie, the goddess who greeted brave warriors in Valhalla after death.
5. Christian cross.

If you visited a Viking town, you might be surprised to see that some houses had a dead (and decaying) animal fixed above the door. These were religious sacrifices, offered to the gods to give thanks for past favours or to ask for future help. Other sacrifices – food, and sometimes people – might be made at holy woods or magic trees in the countryside. Kings, jarls and other powerful men led the rituals on special festival days.

Religion, myths and legends were important in Viking life. They helped people face a harsh and uncertain world with courage and hope. Viking laws and traditional codes of brave and honourable behaviour also helped people live together in communities in the country and in towns.

The Vikings had many gods. People might choose one as a personal guardian, or they might pray to different gods for help with different needs. The god Frey and his sister Freya brought fruitfulness and plenty to farms. Odin was the god of battles; Loki was a trickster. Thor was the god of thunder, strength and metalwork. Vikings believed that he protected ordinary men and women in their everyday lives.

Dead Viking chief

Slave girl

Tent

Funeral of a Viking chief on the shores of the Baltic Sea, as described by Muslim traveller Ibn Fadlan who witnessed it in 922. The dead man was placed in a boat, with rich goods, a slave-girl, a dog, farm animals and horses. Then the boat was burned.

VIKING VALUES

Honour: Vikings fought to defend their home, their leader and their family. It was better to die fighting than to run away. That brought shame and disgrace.

Ruthlessness: Vikings killed anyone dangerous. They also killed sickly babies and frail old people who might become a burden.

Generosity: this was the sign of a noble spirit. Kings and jarls rewarded warriors who fought for them; farmers gave food and shelter to travellers.

Comradeship: no-one could survive without loyal friends. Comrades swore oaths and clasped hands before going on dangerous raids together.

Justice: 'Might is right' the Vikings said. Quarrels could be settled by a duel. But there were also laws to help the community live at peace.

Prayers and sacrifices: in holy sanctuaries, Vikings offered sacrifices (usually dead animals) to carved wooden figures which represented their gods. They hoped that the gods would help them in return.

Vigilance: 'A wise man is never far from his weapons' – or so the Vikings said. Vikings were always ready to face sudden danger from pirates, invaders – or from the wild land in which they lived.

FAMILY LIFE

Weaving implements

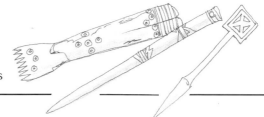

A Woman's Day

6 am Summer sunrise. Gets up. Wakes women slaves. Tells them to fetch water. Gives orders to male slaves who are getting ready to work on the farm.

7 am Supervises senior slave in charge of the milking, and checks on the health of the cows. They are very valuable.

Families, like battle comrades, were very important. Without them, you could not survive. All the members of a family worked together as a team, to make a living and help one another. This loyalty could sometimes lead to bloodshed. If a member of your family was insulted, the oldest men knew it was their duty to fight, and perhaps be killed, to preserve family honour. Children were educated by their family. It was a father's duty to pass on his skills to his sons, and a mother's duty to teach her daughters.

New families were created by marriage. Marriages might be made for love, but, the richer you were, the more likely it would be that your marriage would be arranged. This was an important way of making alliances between powerful people. Brides brought a dowry of money, goods and land, so there were often many men competing to marry rich heiresses, and rich widows, too.

10 am Adds valuable salt to fresh butter to preserve it. In winter, butter and other foods can be stored for months outside in the snow.

11 am Shows her daughter how to make bread, using wheat and barley flour. The dough is kneaded in a big wooden trough.

8 am Time to feed the chickens, geese and pigs. Takes children. They must learn how to care for all the animals.

9 am Checks on work in the dairy. The slaves are churning milk to make butter. It is slow, tiring work.

12 noon Grown-up son arrives with his friends. They have been fishing. Their catch needs to be gutted and salted straight away.

Whalebone ironing board

Heated glass iron
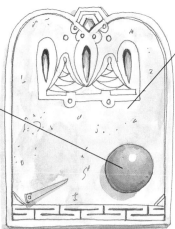

2 pm The slaves bring in the family wash, which has been spread on hedges to dry. The best clothes must be ironed.

Fathers received a 'bride-price' from a bridegroom, but this was worth less than a dowry, because girls were less valued. When times were hard, girl babies might be left out in the open to die, to save the cost of rearing them. Wives had to be faithful, but husbands could take slaves or servants as extra wives. However, women did have some rights. They could divorce a cruel or uncaring husband by making a statement in front of witnesses. They might win respect for their courage and skills. Women were trusted to run farms or businesses while their husbands were abroad. Some fought bravely to drive raiders away from their houses and farms.

4 pm Son has brought firewood to light a big fire on the stone hearth. It is time to start cooking the evening meal.

8 pm dusk Supper time: fish, mutton stew, bread, herbs, fruit and ale. The slaves eat at the other end of the room.

9 pm It is still just light outdoors, and the adults are busy with farmyard tasks. The children are restless.

10 pm Farm work and housework are finished. But there is embroidery, spinning and weaving waiting to be done.

Winter pastimes:
Morels was a game rather like draughts, played with stone or glass counters on a wooden board. This finely-carved board (left) was made in Ireland. Chess became known at the end of the Viking era. These walrus-tusk chessmen (above) were found on the island of Lewis, off the coast of Scotland.

SPORTS AND PASTIMES

In summer, Vikings were busy in workshops and on farms. Days were long, so there was leisure for picnics, swimming, wrestling matches and stallion fights. But in winter, there might be only three or four hours of daylight, and deep snow all around. How, then, did Vikings pass the time?

For women, cooking and cleaning was much the same, though washing and drying clothes (and dirty children) could be difficult. Craftsmen, too, could go on working indoors. Farmers spent daylight hours looking after animals, and mending tools.

Skating was fun, but it was also an important way of getting around. In northern Viking lands, lakes and rivers were frozen for 4 or 5 months every year. Skates were made of polished bone.

Children went swimming in mountain streams, and played on the beaches. They learned to ride horses, if their family was rich. Or they might play a game rather like badminton, with a round wooden bat and feather-filled ball.

If the weather was bright and clear, everyone enjoyed outdoor sports on skis, sledges and skates. These were also used for essential journeys overland. If it was too dark or cold to go outdoors, there were board games such as 'hnefatafl' (like draughts) or gambling, and betting on dice. Most of all, Vikings enjoyed entertaining family and friends with good food and drink, songs and poems, around a roaring fire. Feasts like this could last for several days, with guards posted at the doors to stop enemies attacking while the revellers were drunk. The most important winter feast was Yule (12 January in the modern calendar). It marked the turning point of the year. From then on, the days would begin to brighten and lengthen, and people could look forward to the spring.

Skalds were poets – some travelled around from farm to farm, others lived in the palaces of kings or jarls. They recited dramatic poems about Viking gods, heroes and their adventures. They also played music on the lyre and deer-bone flute.

Viking girls played with dolls. But they also had to learn how to make the cloth to dress them.

Viking men prided themselves on always being ready for battle. Sports like wrestling helped them to stay strong and fit.

Warriors' sons were given toy shields and wooden swords and taught how to fight. Some day, these skills might save their lives.

GOODS FOR SALE

Everything the Vikings used had to be made by hand. There were no big machines to help. Viking farmers made many of the everyday items they needed – such as simple wooden tools. Viking women and girls all knew how to spin thread, weave, and sew. Everyone learned how to do simple repairs. But there were some essential items – such as weapons and iron nails – that ordinary people could not make. There were also many luxury goods on sale that they wished they could afford.

Leather was used for shoes, harnesses and belts. Sometimes, for shoes, the hair was left on for extra warmth. The most expensive type of leather was sometimes embossed – patterned with raised, intricate designs.

Combs were used by men and women to smooth their long hair, and remove lice and fleas. To make one:
(1) Cut small, square-shaped plates of antler.
(2) Cut two longer top pieces, and drill holes in them. (3) Get some iron pins. (4) Drill holes in the square plates.
(5) Assemble the comb, then use a saw to cut the square plates into neatly spaced teeth.

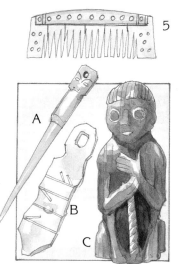

Bones, antlers and teeth (from walruses) were used to make pins (A), name-tags (B), and amulets (C) as well as flutes and chessmen.

Above:
Some amber items.
Below: Pottery imported from Germany.

Fine glass for drinking horns (right) came from the Rhineland in Germany. Patterned glass beads were made by heating and twisting rods of coloured glass.

Craftsmen and women played a vital part in Viking society. Most villages had their local blacksmith, builder and carpenter. But in the towns, specialist craft-workers produced an astonishing range of goods, using local materials like fur and wax or rarities like glass and silver imported from overseas. Visitors to Hedeby could buy bronze brooches, bone combs and hairpins, amulets of walrus ivory, pottery or soapstone bowls, leather harnesses and carved wooden horse-collars, sword-blades from France, amber from the Baltic, silk from China, and Middle Eastern gold. All hand-made goods took a long time to produce, so they were often expensive to buy.

Wealthy Vikings hung beautiful tapestries on their walls, for decoration and extra warmth. This tapestry was found at Oseberg, Norway.

All cloth was made on upright looms. Warp threads were weighted with stones; weft threads were woven in between.

Viking women were skilled at embroidery and at weaving patterned braid – made by passing coloured threads through holes in bone tablets.

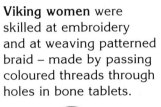

Clothmaking tools:
1. Loom weight.
2. Comb for smoothing wool fibres before spinning.
3. Spindle for spinning thread.
4. Reel for winding thread.
5. Shears for cutting.

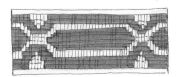

THE METAL WORKSHOP

Every Viking metal-worker knew that lives depended on the weapons he made in his workshop. By law, all Viking men were meant to be ready to defend themselves and their families at any time of the day or night. This was a sensible precaution – who knew when enemies might attack? Viking pirates were feared throughout Europe for frequent, terrifying raids – as one Irish monk reported, only stormy weather kept them in harbour – but they also preyed on their own compatriots, living closer to home. Viking settlements might also be raided by Russians, Slavs or Germans, seeking revenge for past Viking attacks.

Armies were led by jarls or kings. Some-times, workmen from towns were recruited as freelance soldiers, who fought for anyone who could pay. A soldier provided his own weapons and armour – sword, spear, shield and helmet. Rich Vikings fought on horseback, and owned famous swords that had killed many men. Some had names, like 'battle-fire' or 'dragon-bite'. The poorest soldiers could not afford swords. They fought with plain iron axes, catapults and clubs. When the battle was over, all soldiers, rich and poor, looked forward to receiving their share of weapons, clothes, amulets and jewellery, looted from dead bodies on the losing side.

Amulet

Bracelet

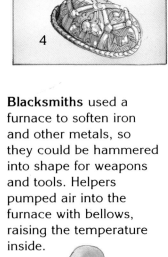

1

2

3

4

Cheap brooches could be mass-produced using as little (expensive) metal as possible:
(1) Press clay on to a good brooch to make the front half of a mould. (2) Line mould with a damp cloth. (3) Cover cloth with more clay to make back half of mould. Remove cloth and pour molten metal into the thin space between two halves of the mould. (4) Leave metal to set, take away mould.

Blacksmiths used a furnace to soften iron and other metals, so they could be hammered into shape for weapons and tools. Helpers pumped air into the furnace with bellows, raising the temperature inside.

Iron ore was plentiful in Sweden. It was smelted (heated with charcoal) to produce iron.

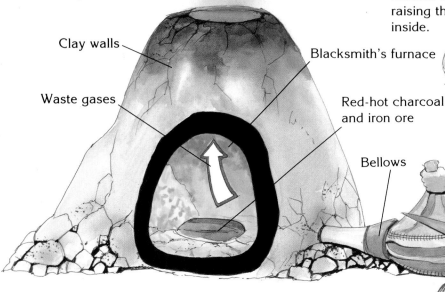

Clay walls

Waste gases

Blacksmith's furnace

Red-hot charcoal and iron ore

Bellows

Anvil

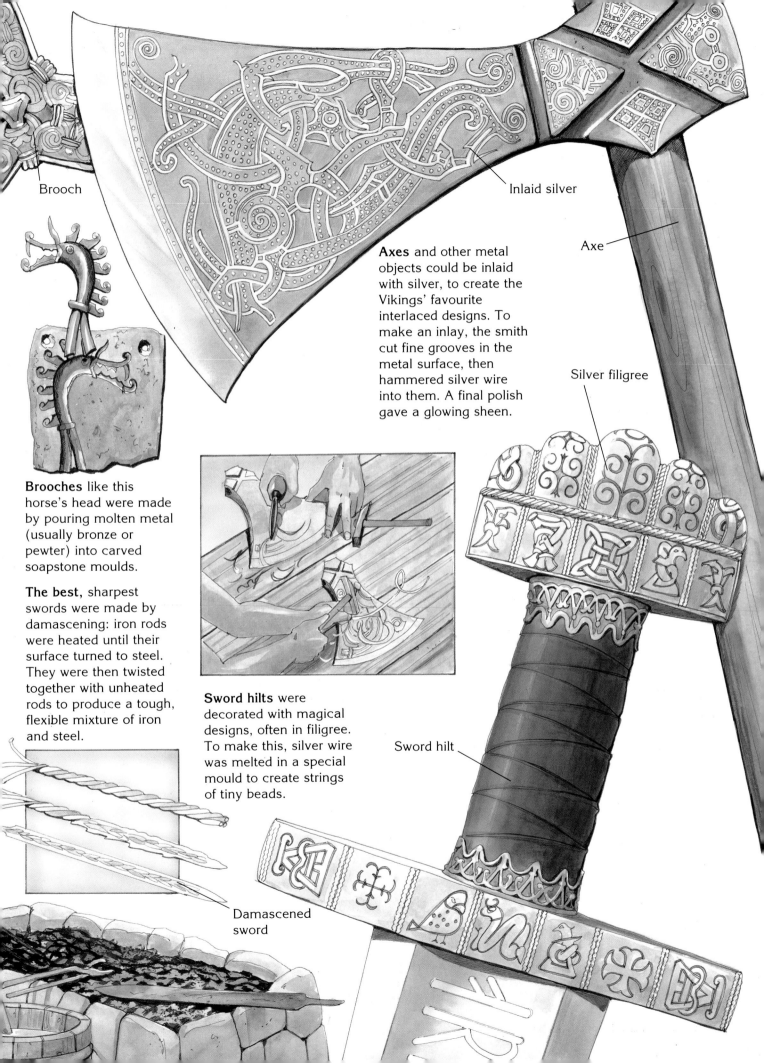

Brooch

Inlaid silver

Axe

Silver filigree

Axes and other metal objects could be inlaid with silver, to create the Vikings' favourite interlaced designs. To make an inlay, the smith cut fine grooves in the metal surface, then hammered silver wire into them. A final polish gave a glowing sheen.

Brooches like this horse's head were made by pouring molten metal (usually bronze or pewter) into carved soapstone moulds.

The best, sharpest swords were made by damascening: iron rods were heated until their surface turned to steel. They were then twisted together with unheated rods to produce a tough, flexible mixture of iron and steel.

Sword hilts were decorated with magical designs, often in filigree. To make this, silver wire was melted in a special mould to create strings of tiny beads.

Sword hilt

Damascened sword

THE SHIPYARD

Travel by sea was a vital part of Viking life, and many Vikings were expert sailors. People depended on ships for raiding, trading, fishing, exploring, and settling in new lands overseas. It was often quicker to travel by boat around the coast than to make long, difficult journeys overland across high mountains or through thick forests. Boats could also carry heavy, bulky loads, such as iron or grain, more easily and cheaply than a horse and cart – the only Viking alternatives. It is not surprising, therefore, that almost all Viking towns were built at the water's edge.

A knorr, or Viking trading ship. Its sturdy hull was wide and deep, designed to provide ample space for cargo.

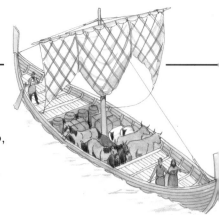

Many towns had shipyards – sheltered, shallow-water bays where boats could be built on the shore and then pushed easily into the water when they were ready to be launched. Viking ships were strong and well made. They were constructed from wood, and powered by a single canvas sail, or by rowers using oars. Ships were different sizes and shapes according to their purpose – warship, coastal ship, or ocean-going trader. Viking shipbuilders did not have plans or drawings to help them; they followed tradition, or were guided by their own training (from a master craftsman), and by what they learned from experienced sailors.

Building a ship. First, the keel was laid down, then the prow and stern-post added. The hull was built of overlapping planks, called strakes, held in place with iron nails. Joins were caulked (sealed) with tarred wool. Inner ribs and cross-pieces were fitted inside the hull for extra strength. Holes were cut along the top for the oars, with covers to keep water out.

Carved wooden animal head

Cross piece

Mastfish (supports mast)

Ribs

Oarhole

Rudder

Cross piece

Ship construction details:

1. Prow and sternpost were joined to the keel by overlapping joints.
2. The mastfish (a large block of wood) held the mast steady.
3. Shields hung on pegs along the hull-side kept sea spray out.
4. Ships were steered by a rudder attached to the stern on the right-hand (starboard) side.
5. Joining strakes for the hull: a metal washer (called a roving) held each nail in place.

Shipbuilding tools:
A. Adze for shaping planks.
B. Axe for chopping.
C. Iron-headed hammer.
D. Wooden mallet.
E. Pincers to remove nails.
F. Auger for boring holes.
G. Saw.
H. Scraper for hollowing and smoothing wood.
I. Chisel for carving.
J. Sharp knife.

Warships were very shallow, so they could land on beaches or sail inland along rivers during raids.

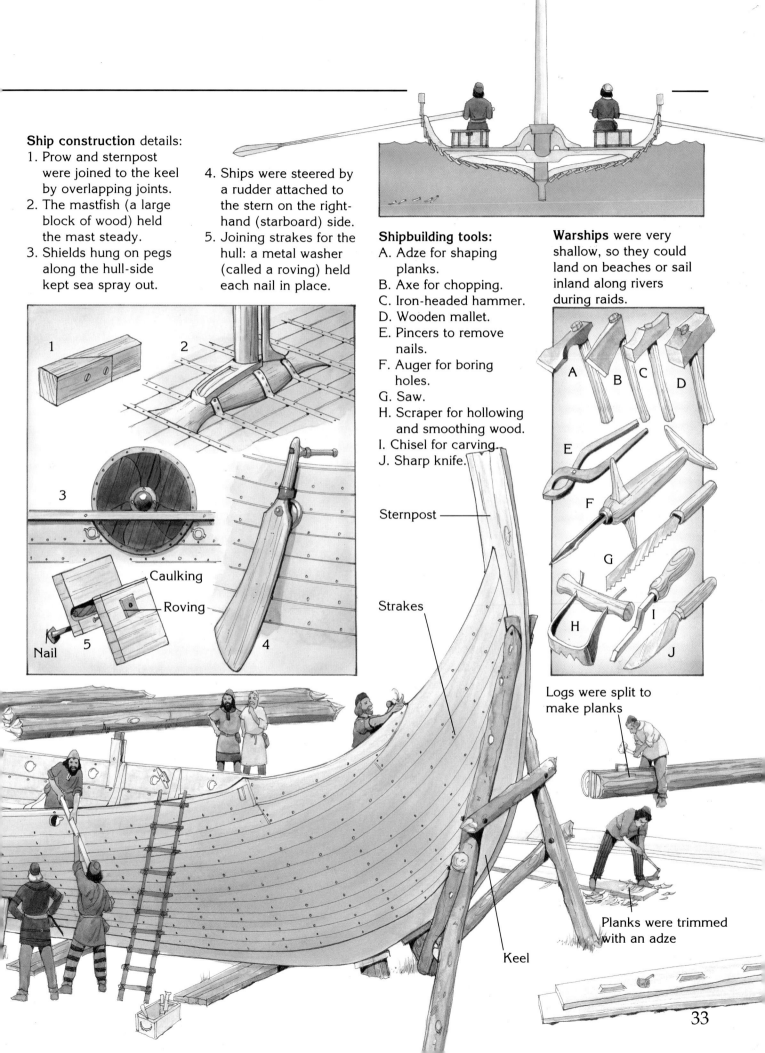

1

2

3

Caulking

Roving

Nail 5

4

Sternpost

Strakes

Keel

A B C D

E

F

G

H I

J

Logs were split to make planks

Planks were trimmed with an adze

33

OVERSEAS TRADE

Down by the harbour, the merchants are busy, watching valuable cargo being loaded on their ships. They are getting ready to set sail on a long voyage – maybe northwards to Iceland and Greenland, or south to the Viking kingdoms in England, Ireland, and Normandy in France. They have all kinds of goods to barter (exchange) for local produce, or even for food and lodgings in foreign lands. Barter was the Viking

In summer, merchants waiting at Hedeby for their ships to be loaded with cargo lived in tents pitched in a field near the waterfront.

Close by the harbour were workshops and stalls where merchants could get their ships repaired and buy provisions for their next voyage.

merchants' preferred way of trading, although they sometimes paid for goods with silver coins. Many Viking towns, including Hedeby and York, had mints, where coins decorated with the proud heads of local rulers were made by skilled craftsmen, known as moneyers.

Once out at sea, how did these Viking merchants know how to steer their ships? They had no maps or charts – after all, most Vikings could not read. But Viking sailors

Riverboat   Ferry

Viking warships were often called 'longships'. Compared with merchant ships, they were very much longer – up to 28 metres in length – and very much narrower, too.

Small rowing boats with auxiliary sails were used by travellers on sheltered fjords, rivers and lakes. Larger ferry-boats carried people and animals to outlying islands or for short trips across the sea.

knew how to work out their position and set a course by carefully monitoring the wind and the waves, and by observing the movements of shoals of fish through the water, or the flight of seabirds overhead. Even the smell of smoke (from cooking fires) and sheep's dung (from the fields) could tell them that they were approaching land, long before it became visible above the horizon.

Viking ships did not have decks with a hold underneath for storage. Each sailor kept his possessions in a strong wooden chest, which he sat on when rowing. In a storm, crew and cargo were covered, where possible, by animal skins.

A MERCHANT'S YEAR

Merchants travelling eastwards from Viking towns might spend a year away from home. It could easily take that long to travel through Russia to Constantinople, where merchants from the Middle East and the Mediterranean met to buy and sell. Journeys like this were only worthwhile if merchants could expect to make high profits. So, as well as valuable northern goods such as furs, amber, honey and wax, they brought large numbers of slaves with them for sale, captured from Germany, the Baltic, and Slav and Russian lands. On their return journey, Vikings carried other profitable items: silks, spices, sweet wines and silver.

A few Vikings ventured even further east, to the shores of the Caspian Sea. There, they met merchants travelling along two great international highways, the 'Silk Route' through Central Asia to China, and the 'Spice Route', to India and beyond.

Set off eastwards from Viking town across the Baltic Sea to Russia. Then sail as far east as you can, across lakes and up the River Dneiper.

In winter, the river will freeze, so you will have to carry the ship. It is quicker to walk on the ice than to struggle through the forests on the river bank.

An ambush by local people – the Petchenegs, who live in the forests.

They know merchants are rich, and want to steal goods and money.

Manage to fight off the ambush, although two men are hurt. But soon reach another river, and sail safely to the great trading city of Kiev. There meet merchants from Asia and the Middle East, who have silks and spices to sell.

Also in Kiev, meet other Vikings, who have built their own settlement there. It is pleasant to relax in Viking style in the warm, steamy bath-house, especially as there is snow outside.

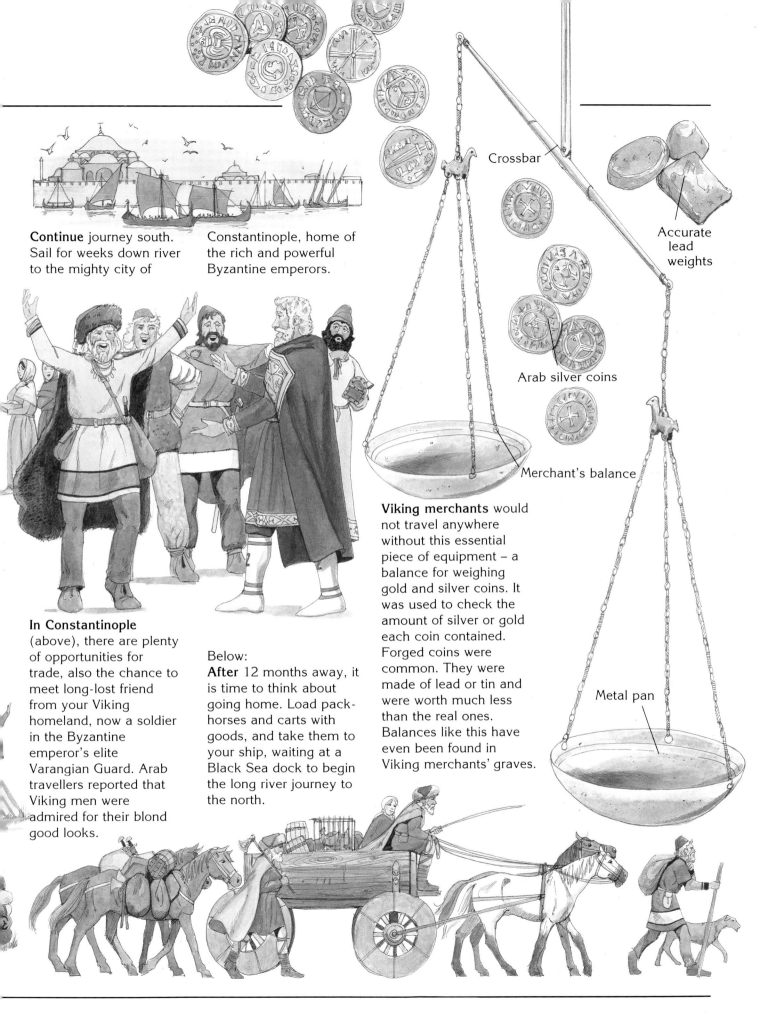

Continue journey south. Sail for weeks down river to the mighty city of Constantinople, home of the rich and powerful Byzantine emperors.

Crossbar

Accurate lead weights

Arab silver coins

Merchant's balance

Viking merchants would not travel anywhere without this essential piece of equipment – a balance for weighing gold and silver coins. It was used to check the amount of silver or gold each coin contained. Forged coins were common. They were made of lead or tin and were worth much less than the real ones. Balances like this have even been found in Viking merchants' graves.

Metal pan

In Constantinople (above), there are plenty of opportunities for trade, also the chance to meet long-lost friend from your Viking homeland, now a soldier in the Byzantine emperor's elite Varangian Guard. Arab travellers reported that Viking men were admired for their blond good looks.

Below:
After 12 months away, it is time to think about going home. Load pack-horses and carts with goods, and take them to your ship, waiting at a Black Sea dock to begin the long river journey to the north.

VIKING RAIDERS

If you lived in Viking times, you would almost certainly know someone – a neighbour or a relative – who went on Viking raids. Going raiding was dangerous – ships might be wrecked, or raiders might be killed during an attack. Vikings were ruthless about injuries; if a comrade didn't recover quickly, he was left to die. His friends could not risk their own lives by staying behind to nurse him. But if raiders survived, they could win lands and riches worth much, much more than anything they could hope to gain by a lifetime of peaceful work, in country or in town.

Raiding was well-organised. Local leaders, usually a jarl or his sons, recruited a band of fit, strong men, who were prepared to leave their homes and set out on an adventure in the hope of winning wealth. Members of this warrior fellowship swore an oath of loyalty to one another, got their weapons together, said goodbye to their families, and sailed away.

Where did raiders go? There were two possible destinations – the rich, well-settled Christian lands to the south, where there

Other European people were so frightened of Viking raids that they wrote special prayers: 'From the terror of the Norsemen, Good Lord deliver us.'

The sight of Viking sails on the horizon inspired terror all along the coasts of Europe. Watchers knew that the 'black birds of prey' (as one French monk called them) would soon attack. Viking warships were designed to sail in shallow water straight up to the shore. Getting off was easy – men and horses just leapt overboard.

The Christian Church opposed slavery. It offered treasures to ransom Christian captives. Kings and local landowners also gave the Vikings money (sometimes called 'danegeld') to stop them attacking their lands. If they didn't pay, the Vikings would start raiding again.

were goods, slaves and treasures to seize, or the remote, almost empty islands to the west – Iceland and Greenland – where there was plenty of land, to raise families, rear livestock and grow crops.

Slaves were captured in Viking raids, and imprisoned by ropes and chains before being led away for transport to the nearest trading town. There they might be sold for money, or bartered for valuable goods.

VIKINGS IN RUSSIA

The northern seas were treacherous during the winter months. The earliest Viking raiders aimed to be safely back in harbour before the storms began. But after around 850, Viking sailors no longer went home in winter. They stayed away - destroying, conquering, trading - for years at a time. They set up winter raiding camps on the Isle of Sheppey in south-east England and at Noirmoutier, in northern France. As one chronicler said, it was 'as if they meant to stay forever'.

Viking raiders and traders also built forts in Russia and the lands bordering the Baltic Sea. These 'temporary' settlements grew into permanent new towns, like Staraja Ladoga in Russia, Grobin in Latvia and Apuole in Lithuania, with log-cabins, market-places, harbours, and stockades. They attracted international traders from many distant lands. But even in these fortified camps, the Vikings knew they were never safe. They were hated by the local Slav peoples, whose young men, women and children they captured to sell as slaves. After dark, Viking merchants and slave-traders only went outside to use the lavatory in armed groups of four. While one man relieved himself, the others kept guard.

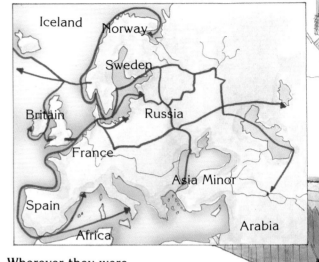

Wherever they were, Viking towns soon became centres of profitable trade.

Viking towns shared many common features, wherever they were built. As in the Viking homelands, most houses were built of wood. The Vikings always feared attack – either from other Vikings anxious to seize their goods, or from hostile local people, angry to have Viking settlers living on their land.

Traded in Viking towns:
1. Bracelet made from Middle Eastern gold.
2. Furs from Russia, Iceland and Norway.
3. Gold brooches made by Viking craftworkers.
4. Silver from Germany.
5. Silk from China.
6. Swords from Germany.
7. Brazier from Baghdad.
8. Rhineland glass.
9. Middle Eastern glass.
10. Indian spices.
11. Persian pottery.
12. Viking glass beads.
13. Arabic silver coins.

New Viking Settlements

The first inhabitants of overseas Viking forts and camps were men – with perhaps a few captive slave girls to look after them. These Viking warriors spent their time plundering and collecting tribute. But gradually, farmers and traders followed the raiders, attracted by new opportunities, or the hope of more land.

Many peaceful Vikings decided to leave their old homes in Scandinavia and settle in these territories, now under Viking control. Their wives and children joined them, and new Viking communities were formed – for example, at Dublin and York. Sadly, migrants were sometimes overtaken by disaster. Of 250 ships that left Iceland in 986, carrying settlers for Greenland, only 14 arrived.

Everywhere, Viking kings, jarls and officials began to organise these new kingdoms, and all the different peoples who lived there. They collected taxes, enforced laws and minted coins. Viking language and customs mingled with local traditions, to create new lifestyles.

New towns could also be built in Viking homelands. In 10th-century Denmark, King Harald Bluetooth built Trelleborg and three other fortified settlements as centres of government and monuments to royal power.

(Below) **After** about 860, Viking settlers built new villages in Iceland. There were no trees to provide timber, so houses were built on stone foundations with thick walls of rammed earth and turf. After about 986, new Viking settlements were built in southern Greenland, too.

(Above) **Viking** slave merchants often spent months or years trading in Russia and other Slav lands. To protect themselves from hostile local peoples, they built well-defended forts.

Some Viking merchants did not reach home safely. They died or were killed abroad. Their friends left memorial stones for them, decorated with Viking patterns and runes, in many parts of the Viking world.

Viking finds at York:
1. Leatherworking tools.
2. Wooden lavatory seat.
3. Leather boot.
4. Metal helmet.
5. Loom weights.
6. Bone pins.
7. Wooden spindle.
8. Horn spoon.
9. Silver coins.
10. Antler comb.
11. Wooden bowl.
12. Jet cross.
13. Silver brooches.
14. Pottery storage jar.

In Britain, Viking kings ruled from thriving towns like York (Viking name: Yorvik). Archaeologists have found many Viking objects there.

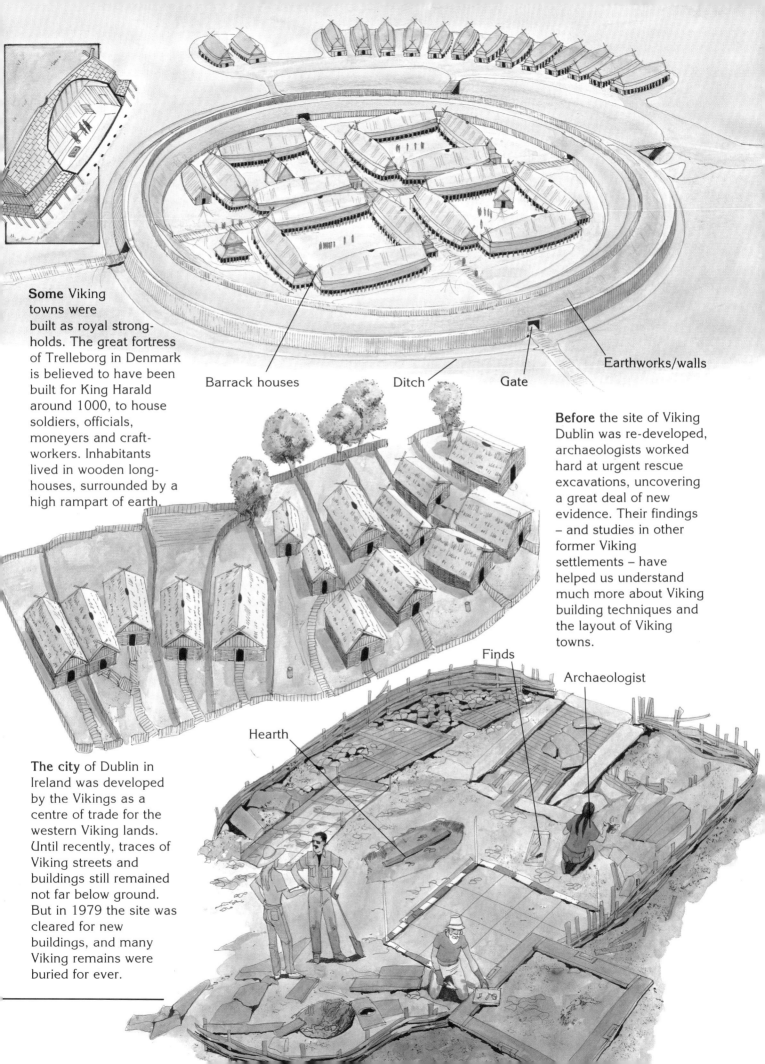

Some Viking towns were built as royal strongholds. The great fortress of Trelleborg in Denmark is believed to have been built for King Harald around 1000, to house soldiers, officials, moneyers and craftworkers. Inhabitants lived in wooden longhouses, surrounded by a high rampart of earth.

Barrack houses

Ditch

Gate

Earthworks/walls

Before the site of Viking Dublin was re-developed, archaeologists worked hard at urgent rescue excavations, uncovering a great deal of new evidence. Their findings – and studies in other former Viking settlements – have helped us understand much more about Viking building techniques and the layout of Viking towns.

Finds

Archaeologist

Hearth

The city of Dublin in Ireland was developed by the Vikings as a centre of trade for the western Viking lands. Until recently, traces of Viking streets and buildings still remained not far below ground. But in 1979 the site was cleared for new buildings, and many Viking remains were buried for ever.

VIKING TIMELINE

*c.*500–*c.*700 The Vendel Period (pre-Viking era) in Scandinavia.

600–700 Swedish merchants and sailors set up colonies along the shores of the Baltic Sea.

700–800 First Viking raids by Norwegian sailors on neighbouring western countries. They need more land to grow crops to feed a growing population. Some hope to get rich quickly by seizing treasure. A few want to get away away from the watchful control of increasingly-powerful Norwegian kings.

793 Viking raiders from Norway attack and destroy the Christian monastery of Lindisfarne, off the north-eastern coast of England.

795 Viking raiders attack the monastery of St Columba, on Iona, an island off the west coast of Scotland.

800 Viking raiders from Norway set up camps in Orkney and Shetland, and in the Faeroe Islands (off Denmark). They prepare to invade Ireland.

808 King Godfred of Denmark founds new town at Hedeby.

827 Christian missionary Ansgar preaches in Hedeby, but does not make many converts.

828 Vikings invade Ireland and seize control.

834 Vikings from Denmark attack the great trading centre at Dorestad on the Rhine.

835 Danish Vikings raid Sheppey, a small island close to the south-east English coast.

841 The first Viking settlers (from Norway) arrive in Ireland; they establish the city of Dublin.

841 Danish Vikings sail up the river Seine to raid the important French town of Rouen.

843 Danish Vikings attack the French port of Nantes and terrorise the surrounding countryside. They destroy many monasteries, villages and farms.

844 Viking raiders sail south and attack Seville, in Spain. They are driven out by Spain's Muslim rulers.

845 Vikings attack Paris, capital city of France. King Charles the Bald of France offers them money (called 'Danegeld') to go away. From now on, Viking raiders in England and France demand huge payments every year.

850 For the first time, Viking raiders stay in England all winter.

859 Vikings sail to the Mediterranean, where they live as pirates for three years.

860–874 Vikings begin to settle in Iceland.

862 Rurik the Viking founds trading city of Novgorod in Russia.

866 The Vikings capture York and set up a kingdom there.

*c.*870 Vikings control most of eastern England – known as the 'Danelaw'.

871 King Alfred of Wessex leads the English resistance to the Vikings. He insists that the Viking leaders become Christian.

886 Vikings and English make peace.

*c.*900 Vikings establish trade routes overland through Russia.

*c.*900 King Harald Bluetooth of Denmark orders strong outer rampart to be built to protect Hedeby from raiders.

911 Viking leader Rollo sets up Viking kingdom in Normandy in western France. He also promises to help defend France.

960 King Harald Bluetooth of Denmark becomes a Christian, and encourages his subjects to follow his example.

980 Vikings launch new series of raids on England.

*c.*982 Viking Erik the Red lands in Greenland for the first time.

994 King Olaf Tryggvason of Norway and King Svein Forkbeard of Denmark lead fleet of 94 ships to attack London.

*c.*1000 Leif Eriksson reaches America.

1013 King Svein Forkbeard invades England.

1017 King Svein controls England. After his death, his son, Cnut, rules. He is also ruler of a great Scandinavian empire in Norway, Denmark and Sweden.

1035 King Cnut dies.

1042 King Edward the Confessor regains control of England from Vikings.

1050 Hedeby attacked and burned by Norwegian Vikings.

1066 Hedeby destroyed by the Wends (a Slav nation living beside the Baltic Sea).

1066 King Harald Hardrada of Norway invades England. He is killed at the Battle of Stamford Bridge, near York.

1066 The Normans (who are descendants of Rollo of Normandy and his fellow Vikings) invade and conquer England, led by their ruler, Duke William.

1071 Vikings capture Sicily and southern Italy and establish a kingdom there.

1100 The end of the Viking age. Viking settlers in various European lands are now integrated with local people.

GLOSSARY

Adze, wood-working tool with a sharp blade, used for shaping and trimming strakes (see opposite page).

Amulet, small object, like a lucky charm, believed to keep evil away.

Auger, woodworking tool, used to bore holes.

Battens, thin strips of wood.

Blubber, thick layer of fat beneath the skin of seals and whales.

Buttermilk, a drink made from deliberately-soured milk, rather like thin yoghurt.

Caulked, padded with rope and tar to keep water out.

Damascening, metal-working technique in which iron and steel were combined to form a strong, flexible alloy.

Danegeld, tax collected by Viking warriors from the kings of England and France. If it was not paid, the Vikings threatened to attack.

Danelaw, area of England ruled by the Vikings during the 9th and 10th centuries.

Daub, mud, straw and horsehair, mixed together and used with wattle (see below) to make walls).

Embossed, decorated with a raised pattern.

Filigree, a fine, delicate decoration for metalwork, made from heated gold and silver wire, or from tiny droplets of gold and silver.

Fjords, deep bays running inland from the sea, with mountain slopes on either side.

Jarl, powerful Viking landowner and local leader or nobleman.

Keel, heavy wooden beam at the base of a ship.

Knorr, wide-bodied Viking trading ship.

Lyre, musical instrument with strings, rather like a small harp.

Mastfish, large, strong, fish-shaped block of wood used to support the mast in Viking ships.

Merels, board game, rather like draughts.

Missionary, someone sent to another country to teach the local inhabitants about a new religious faith.

Mole, a harbour wall.

Molten, heated and melted.

Pagan, belonging to a religion that is not Christian, Muslim or Jewish.

Palisade, wall made of thick tree trunks driven into the ground.

Piles, posts sunk into the ground, to act as foundations for buildings.

Port (of ships), the left-hand side of a ship, facing towards the prow (front).

Prow, the front end of a ship.

Quern, hand-operated machine for grinding grain into flour, made out of two heavy stones. The top one moved round, crushing grains against the lower one.

Rammed, packed down tightly.

Roving, metal washer fixed to the end of metal nails to hold them firmly in place. The end of each nail was bent over and hammered flat against the roving.

Rudder, large paddle fixed to the rear of a boat, and used for steering.

Runes, the letters of the Viking alphabet. Used for writing and carving, and also for casting spells.

Skald, professional poet and musician.

Soapstone, a soft-textured stone that can easily be carved.

Starboard, the right-hand side of a ship, facing towards the prow (front).

Stern, the back end of a ship.

Strakes, long planks, used to make the hull of a ship.

Valhalla, a place like heaven, where Viking warriors went after death.

Valkyrie, fierce female goddesses or spirits, who welcomed the souls of dead warriors into Valhalla. Said to be the nine daughters of the Viking god Odin.

Vendel, the culture that flourished in Scandinavia for approximately 200 years before the Viking age. It is named after archaeological finds made at the village of Vende in Sweden.

Vinland, the first-known Viking settlement in America, in present-day Newfoundland.

Warp, the lengthways (end-to-end) threads of a piece of cloth. In an upright Viking loom they hung downwards, held in place by heavy weights. The weft threads were woven across them.

Wattle, dry twigs, woven together. Usually smeared with daub (mud, straw and horse-hair) to make walls.

Weft, the crosswise threads in a piece of cloth, woven in and out of the lengthwise warp threads.

Winter solstice, the shortest day of the year. In the northern hemisphere, 21st December.

Zoned, divided into separate areas.

INDEX

Page numbers in bold refer to illustrations.